WWW.ZODIACSERVICES.NET

Presents

MBA BASICS IN 24 HOURS!

A SIMPLE HANDBOOK OF MASTERS IN BUSINESS ADMINISTRATION

ADDITIONAL BOOK 1 – GLOBAL MARKETING AND FOREIGN TRADE MANAGEMENT

Life Grows With Us!

SIMPLE & EASY WAY TO UNDERSTAND THE BASICS OF BUSINESS ADMINISTRATION TOPICS EASILY IN SUMMARY AND KEYWORDS WITH 8 EFFECTIVE CHAPTERS & ADDITIONAL TOPICS!

By

G.R. Narasimhan

Welcome to Zodiac Services MBA chapters in brief with eight effective and additional special topics given as individual books!

I0405843

GOOD LUCK TO BE A BUSINESS ADMINISTRATOR!

Zodiac Services, Chennai, India

Get more contact details and numbers from:

www.zodiacservices.net [or] mail to info@zodiacservices.net

Ordering Information for hardcopies:

Quantity sales – Special discounts are available on quantity purchases by corporations, associations and others. For details, contact the author at the address above.

JUNE 2019 – First Edition

Released and Published in India

ABOUT THE AUTHOR

G.R. Narasimhan – Sr. Consultant for technology and business under **Zodiac Services Chennai** (as on June 2019) which was started in 2010 to serve the people in alternative beliefs/therapies like astrological predictions, prayers, remedies, prasanam (divine words) and vedic guidance for short- or long-term problems, vaastu, numerology, gem stones, yantras, mantras or rituals (related areas), yoga, meditation, counselling and alternative therapies consulting. Business & education, soft skills/software/electronics & communication training & promotion, web designing, career counselling and Internet & social media marketing are additionally served. Assisting the entrepreneurship business for the above mentioned areas to serve better for the clients, **G.R. Narasimhan** also the author of few e-books called 'A Simple guide to Vedic Astrology', 'Inverted Universal Meditation & Engineering', 'Secrets of Equity Stocks to make Millions', 'Symbolic Meditation & Developing ESP' and many other (are already available in Amazon) having extended experience in IT + Management areas developed website and online marketing using different business strategies and continue the service very well to extend further including this 'MBA Basics in 24 Hours with Additional Topics – Global Marketing and Foreign Trade' – concepts specifically based on the business administration topics applied overall in the academic curriculum. With the continuous extraordinary ability and skills in research and experience, he is able to explain and train/assist others with extended support and guidance by counselling/consulting effectively.

Great thanks and good luck for everyone reading this book on 'MBA Basics in 24 Hours' with almost all the areas of basic business administration or career growth individually or as a group. For any queries and feedback, you can contact directly via email to info@zodiacservices.net, info@astroservices.in or astronara@gmail.com.

CONTENTS

Topic	Page Numbers

INTRODUCTION — 5

PART 1 – GLOBAL MARKETING MANAGEMENT

[Chapter One] – Introduction to Global Marketing — 7

[Chapter Two] – The Global Economic Environment — 8

[Chapter Three] – Social and Cultural Environment — 9

[Chapter Four] – The Political, Legal and Regulatory Environments of Global Marketing — 10

[Chapter Five] – Global Customers — 11

[Chapter Six] – Global Marketing Information Systems & Research — 12

[Chapter Seven] – Segmentation, Targeting and Positioning — 13

[Chapter Eight] – Entry and Expansion Strategies: Marketing and Sourcing — 14

[Chapter Nine] – Cooperative Strategies & Global Strategic Partnerships — 16

[Chapter Ten] – Competitive Analysis and Strategy — 17

[Chapter Eleven] – Product Decisions — 18

[Chapter Twelve] – Pricing Decisions — 19

[Chapter Thirteen] – Global Marketing Channels & Physical Distribution — 20

[Chapter Fourteen] – Global Advertising — 21

[Chapter Fifteen] – Global Promotion — 22

[Chapter Sixteen] – Global E-Marketing — 23

[Chapter Seventeen] – Leading, Organising and Monitoring the Global Marketing Effort — 24

[Chapter Eighteen] – The Future of Global Marketing — 25

PART 2 – FOREIGN EXCHANGE MANAGEMENT

[Chapter One] – International Monetary System — 26

[Chapter Two] – Foreign Exchange Market — 27

[Chapter Three] – Exchange Rate Determination — 28

[Chapter Four] – Exchange Rate Forecasting — 29

[Chapter Five] – Introduction to Exchange Risk — 30

[Chapter Six] – Management of Exchange Risk — 31

CONCLUSION — 32

INTRODUCTION

Business Administration is the combination of different areas of skills in management. Managing and maintaining several departments or areas of activities described in a single umbrella or vertical called management of business administration. The following areas are the main topics or chapters for the discussion under business administration, mostly common for any bachelors or masters studies.

- Principles & Practices of Management
- Human Resource Management
- Financial Management
- Marketing Management
- Organisational Behaviour
- Managerial Economics
- Strategic Management
- Management Information Systems

Then there are several branches extended in business administration like foreign trade, global marketing, international business, social work, information technology, finance, human resources etc. These above eight topics considered to summarise and define important brief summary and keywords under which various chapters for each topic are given (published in Amazon).

This book covers the summaries and definitions of keywords for the topic 'Global Marketing and Foreign Trade Management' with the following chapters.

Introduction to Global Marketing, The Global Economic Environment, Social and Cultural Environment, The Political, Legal and Regulatory Environments of Global Marketing, Global Customers, Global Marketing Information Systems & Research, Segmentation, Targeting and Positioning, Entry and Expansion Strategies: Marketing and Sourcing, Cooperative Strategies & Global Strategic Partnerships, Competitive Analysis and Strategy, Product Decisions, Pricing Decisions, Global Marketing Channels & Physical Distribution, Global Advertising, Global Promotion, Global E-Marketing, Leading, Organising and Monitoring the Global Marketing Effort & The Future of Global Marketing, International Monetary System, Foreign Exchange Market, Exchange Rate Determination, Exchange Rate Forecasting, Introduction to Exchange Risk and Management of Exchange Risk.

Some of the chapters given with examples of Indian economy/trading related terms. But readers must understand the concepts of their own country's business & economy and other areas.

As it has high level of contents in brief which can be covered in three hours maximum, readers can read other books from different authors to gain in-depth knowledge of the given business management and administration. This book gives quick glance & easy go chapters for any situation like interview, short answering and overall explanation to present others. Good Luck!

PART 1 – GLOBAL MARKETING MANAGEMENT
[Chapter One] – Introduction to Global Marketing

- Global marketing is the process of focusing the resources and objectives of a company on global marketing opportunities.

- Companies engage in global marketing for two reasons: to take advantage of opportunities for growth and expansion and to survive. Companies that fail to pursue global opportunities are likely to lose their domestic markets because they will be pushed aside by stronger and more competitive global competitors.

- This represents the theory and practice of applying the universal discipline of marketing to the global opportunities found in the world markets.

- The basic goals of marketing are to create customer value and competitive advantage by maintaining focus.

- Company management can be classified in terms of its orientation towards the world: ethnocentric orientation characterises domestic and international companies and international companies pursue marketing outside the home market by extending various element of the marketing mix.

- A polycentric worldview predominates at a multinational company, where the marketing mix is adapted by country managers operating autonomously.

- Managers at global and transnational companies are region-centric or geocentric in their orientation and pursue both extension and adaptation strategies in global markets.

- Global marketing's importance today is shaped by the dynamic interplay of several driving and restraining forces. The former include market needs and wants, technology, transportation improvements, costs, quality, global peace, world economic growth and recognition of opportunities to develop leverage by operating globally.

- Restraining forces include market differences, management myopia, organisational culture and national controls.

[Chapter Two] – The Global Economic Environment

- The economic environment is a major determinant of global market potential and opportunity.

- The world's economies can be categorised as market allocation systems, command allocation systems and mixed system. A major trend in recent years has been the transition towards market economies in many countries that had been centrally controlled.

- Countries can be categorised in terms of their stage of economic development: low income, lower- middle income, upper-middle income, high income and basket cases.

- It is possible to identify distinct stages and formulate general estimates about the type of demand associated with a particular stage of development.

- For many products, the single most important indicator of market potential is income; therefore, the first step in determining the potential of a country or region is to be identifying the total and per capita income.

- Market potential for a product can be evaluated by determining product saturation levels in light of income levels. In general, it is appropriate to compare the saturation levels of countries or of consumer segments with similar income levels.

- Balance-of-payments issues are also important economic considerations. The U.S. merchandise trade deficit has passed the $100 billion mark several times in recent years; the United States is thus a debtor; Japan enjoys a trade surplus and serves a creditor nation.

- One of the ways of dealing with the complexity of a world with over 200 national markets is to focus on economic cooperation agreements.

- Examples: The European Union is bringing down trade barriers in Europe not only amongst the 15 member countries but also with the countries of Central and Eastern Europe. NAFTA has created a free-trade area encompassing Canada, the United States and Mexico. In the Asia- Pacific region, ASEAN is expanding and eliminating trade barriers in that region. Mercosur, the Andean Group, CACM and CARICOM are the four economic cooperation agreements in Central and South America.

[Chapter Three] – Social and Cultural Environment

- Culture, a society's 'a programming of the mind', has both a pervasive and changing influence on each national market environment.

- Global marketers must recognise the influence of culture on all aspects of life including work habits and consumption of products.

- Human behaviour is a function both of a person's own unique personality and that of person's interaction with the collective forces of the particular society and culture in which he or she has lived.

- A number of concepts can help guide anyone seeking insight into cultural issues. Nations can be classified as high and low context cultures and communication and negotiation styles can differ from country to country. Maslow's hierarchy, Hofstede's typology and the self-reference criterion can provide clues about certain cultural differences and similarities.

- Global marketing has played an important – even leading – role in influencing the rate of cultural change around the world. This is particularly true of food, but it includes virtually every industry, particularly in communication and consumer products.

- The Internet and global television have changed washing habits, the electronics industry has changed entertainment patterns, clothing and marketers have changed styles and so on.

- Although culture can also affect characteristics of industrial products, it is more important as an influence on the marketing process, particularly in the way business is conducted.

- Global marketers have learned to rely on people who know and understand local customs attitudes for marketing expertise.

- Even so, many persons doing business in a new culture avail themselves of training opportunities to help avoid potential cross-cultural complications.

[Chapter Four] – The Political, Legal and Regulatory Environments of Global Marketing

- The legal and political environment of global marketing is the set of governmental institutions, political parties and organisations that are the expression of the people in the nations of the world.

- In particular, anyone engaged in global marketing should have an overall understanding of the importance of sovereignty to national governments.

- The political environment varies from country to country and risk assessment is crucial.

- It is also important to understand a particular government's actions with taxes, dilution of equity control and expropriation.

- The legal environment consists of laws, courts, attorneys and legal customs practices. The countries of the world can be broadly categorised in terms of common law system or code (civil) law system.

- The United States, United Kingdom and the British Commonwealth countries, which include Canada, Australia, New Zealand and the former British Colonies in Africa and India, are common law countries; other countries are based on code law.

- Some of the most important legal issues pertaining to establishment are jurisdiction, patents and trademarks, licensing, antitrust and bribery. When legal conflicts arise, companies can pursue the matter in court or use arbitration.

- The regulatory environment consists of agencies, both governmental and non-governmental, that enforce laws or set guidelines for conducting business.

- Global marketing activities can be affected by a number of international or regional economic organisations; in Europe, for example, the European Union makes laws governing member states. The WTO will have broad impact on global marketing activities in the years to come.

- Although these three environments are complex, astute marketers plan ahead to avoid situations that might result in conflict, misunderstanding or outright violation of national laws.

[Chapter Five] – Global Customers

- Most striking facts about world markets and buyers are that for the first time in modern history, the entire world is growing.

- According to World Bank estimates, every world region including Africa will grow, and for the most part, the poor countries will grow faster than rich.

- This will provide new opportunities for marketers who despite increasing globalisation need to look at the characteristics of each new market they plan to enter or expand.

[Chapter Six] – Global Marketing Information Systems & Research

- Information is one of the most basic ingredients of a successful marketing strategy. The global marketer must scan the world for information about opportunities and threats and make information available via a management information system.

- Scanning can be accomplished by keeping in touch with an area of interest via surveillance or by actively seeking out information via search. Information can be obtained from human and documentary sources or from direct perception.

- Formal research is often required before decisions can be made regarding specific problems or opportunities.

- After developing a research plan, data are collected using either primary or secondary sources.

- A number of techniques are available analysing data, including demand pattern analysis, income elasticity measurements, estimation by analogy, comparative analysis and cluster analysis.

- Research findings must be presented clearly to facilitate decision making. Global marketing research presents a number of challenges.

- First is the simple fact that research on a number of markets may be required, some of which are so small that only modest research expenditure can be made.

- Secondary data from some countries may be distorted and also comparability may be an issue.

- A final issue is how much control headquarters will have over research and the overall management of the organisation's information system.

[Chapter Seven] – Segmentation, Targeting and Positioning

- The global environment must be analysed before a company pursues into new geographic markets.

- Through global market segmentation, the similarities and differences of potential buying customers can be identified and grouped.

- Demographics, psychographics behavioural characteristics and benefits sought are common attributes used to segment world markets. After marketers have identified segments, the next step is targeting.

- The identified groups are evaluated and compared; the prospect(s) with the great potential is selected from them. The groups are evaluated on the several factors: segment size and growth potential, competition and compatibility and feasibility.

- After evaluating the identified segments, marketers must decide on an appropriate targeting strategy.

- The three basic categories of global target marketing strategies are standardised marketing, concentrated marketing and differentiated marketing.

- Finally, companies must plan a way to reach their chosen target market(s) by determining the best positioning for their product offerings. Here, marketers devise an appropriate marketing mix to fix the product in the mind of potential buyers in the target market.

- High-tech and high-touch positioning are two strategies that can work well for a global product.

[Chapter Eight] – Entry and Expansion Strategies: Marketing and Sourcing

- Companies can choose from amongst a wide range of alternatives when deciding how to participate in markets around the world.

- Exporting, licensing, joint venture and ownership each represent distinct advantages and disadvantages.

- The choice depends in part on how a firm configures its value chain. Exporting can help a company build volume and achieve scale economics.

- If a country's currency is weak relative to currencies of trading partners, export sales should be emphasised.

- Licensing is a good strategy for increasing the bottom line with little investment; it can be a good choice for a company with advanced technology or a strong brand image.

- Joint ventures, the third strategic alternative, offer companies the opportunity to share risk and combine value chain strengths. Companies considering joint ventures must plan carefully and communicate with partners to avoid 'divorce'.

- Ownership through start-up or acquisition can require a major commitment of resources. Acquisition offers the benefits of full control and an opportunity to blend technologies.

- Market expansion strategies can be represented in matrix form to assist managers in thinking through the various alternatives.

- The options include country and market concentration, country concentration and market diversification; country preferred expansion strategy will be a reflection of a company's stage of development.

- An international company will use exporting and licensing to exploit headquarters knowledge through worldwide diffusion of products.

- Multinational companies will respond to local differences using acquisitions and manufacturing start-ups in various countries.

- Global companies will either export products around the globe from world-scale plants or will rely on the world for resources.

- The stage 5 transitional combines the strengths of these three stages into an integrated network to leverage worldwide learning.

- It provides an overview of export marketing and the decisions company personnel have to make to become successful exporters. Governments exert a strong influence on exports, through support programs, regulations, nontariff barriers and tariff classifications.

- In choosing export markets, companies must assess market potential, market access, shipping costs, competition, product fit and service requirements. It is definitely a good idea to visit a potential market before developing an export program.

- Market access considerations are particularly important for exporters and the importer. Exporter must understand how tariffs and duties affect the price that must be paid by the importers.

- Supporters exporting entail organisational decisions (e.g. regarding internal or external expertise) in both the manufacturer's country and the market country.

- Exporters and importers must also have a thorough understanding of international financial instruments, especially letters of credit.

- Barter and countertrade are methods of making sales to customers who do not have access to hard currency but are prepared to make payment in some form other than money.

- Changes in the political, economic, sociocultural and technological environments are leading to new strategies in global competition.

- Cooperative strategies, including GSPs and the Japanese keiretsu, have become more important as companies need to share the high cost of product development, pool skills and know how, gain access to markets and find new opportunities for organisational learning.

- GSPs are distinguished by six attributes: They represent long term strategies for achieving global leadership; they involve reciprocal relationships; the partner's vision is truly global, extending beyond home markets; they involve continual lateral transfer of resources; if the partnership is along vertical lines, both parties must be able to defend their competitive position against a partner's forward or backward integration move and the partners retain their identities in markets not included in the partnership.

- Six factors are critical to the success of a GSP: mission, strategy, governance, culture, organisation and management.

- Keiretsu have had enormous significance for the success of Japanese companies, both in Japan and the rest of the world.

- In the United States, the drawing of the digital age is resulting in Keiretsu-style alliances amongst companies in the computer, telecommunications and entertainment industries.

- At the same time, some alliances are resulting in the creation of the virtual corporation, an organisation that exists solely in the network of linkages amongst partners.

[Chapter Ten] – Competitive Analysis and Strategy

- According to Porter's five forces model, industry competition is a function of the threat of new entrants, the threat of substitutes, the bargaining power of suppliers and buyers and rivalry amongst existing competitors.

- Porter's strategic positions can be used by managers to understand how to combine activities to create unique value, the source of competitive advantage.

- Hamel and Prahalad have proposed an alternative framework for pursuing competitive advantage growing out of a firm's strategic intent and use of competitive innovation.

- A firm can build layers of advantage, search for loose bricks in competitors and utilise the technology and know-how. This framework is not necessarily inconsistent with the positions proposed by Porter.

- The concepts proposed by Hamel and Prahalad, as well as D'Aveni, stress the dynamic environment. Strategic positions have shorter lives than in the past and may have to be supplemented or abandoned faster than ever before.

- Today, many companies are discovering that industry competition is changing from purely domestic to a global phenomenon. Thus, competitive analysis must also be carried out on a global scale.

- Global marketers must also have an understanding of national sources. Demand conditions include the composition size and growth pattern of home demand. The rate of home-market growth and the means by which a nation's product are pulled into foreign markets also affect demand conditions.

- The final two determinants are the presence of related and supporting industries and the nature of firm strategy, structure and rivalry. Porter notes that chance and government also influence a nation's competitive advantage.

[Chapter Eleven] – Product Decisions

- The product is the most important element of a marketing program. Global marketers face the challenge of formulating a coherent global product strategy for their companies.

- Product strategy requires an evaluation of the basic needs and conditions of use in the company's existing and proposed markets. Whenever possible, opportunities to market global products should be given precedence over opportunities to market local or international products.

- The same positioning and marketing approaches can be used with global brands such as Coca-Cola.

- Marketers must consider four factors when designing products for global markets: preferences, costs, regulations and compatibility. Attitudes towards a product's country of origin must also be taken into account.

- Three strategic alternatives are open to companies pursuing geographic expansion: product/ communications extension; dual adaptation and product invention. Global competition has created pressure on companies to excel at product development.

- There are different definitions of what constitutes a new product; the most difficult type of new product launch is clearly one involving an entirely new product in a market in which a company has a little or no experience. Successful global product launches require leverage.

- An organisation must accumulate and disseminate knowledge concerning past practices – both successful and unsuccessful. Opportunities for comparative analysis further enhance the effectiveness of marketing planning activities within the global system.

[Chapter Twelve] – Pricing Decisions

- Pricing decisions are a critical element of the marketing mix that must reflect cost and competitive factors. There is no absolute maximum price, but for any customer, price must correspond to the customer's perceived value of the product.

- The aim of most marketing strategies is to set a price that corresponds to customer's perception of value in the product and at the same time does not 'leave money on the table' (i.e. a set of price that is lower than consumers are willing to pay for a product or service).

- Generally, a company must charge for profit in the process. Pricing strategies include market skimming, market penetration and market holding.

- Pricing decisions must also take into account the price escalation that occurs when products are shipped from one country to another.

- International pricing is complicated by the fact that businesses must conform to different laws and different competitive situations in each country.

- Each company must examine the market, the competition and its own costs and objectives and local and regional regulations and laws in setting prices that are consistent with the overall marketing strategy.

- Dumping – selling products in international markets at prices below those in the home country or below the cost of production – and parallel importing are two particularly contentious pricing issues.

- Company managers must also set transfer prices that are appropriate to company profitability objectives and that also conform to tax regulations in individual country markets.

[Chapter Thirteen] – Global Marketing Channels & Physical Distribution

- Channel decisions are difficult to manage globally because of the variation in channel structures from country to country. Nevertheless, certain patterns of change associated with market development offer the astute global marketer the opportunity to create channel innovations and gain competitive advantage.

- The characteristics of customers products, middlemen and environment all impact channel design and strategy.

- Consumer channels may be direct, via mail or door to door; the Internet or direct factory / manufacturer outlets or they may involve one or more levels or resellers. A combination of the manufacturer's salespeople, wholesalers and dealers or agents is being utilised.

- In developed countries, retail channels are characterised by the substitution of capital for labour. This is evident in self-service stores, which offer a wide range of items at relatively low gross margins.

- The opposite is true in less developed countries with abundant labour. Such countries disguise their unemployment in inefficient retail and wholesale channels suited to the needs of consumers; such channels may have gross margins that are 50 per cent lower than those in self-service stores in developed countries.

- A global marketer must either tailor the marketing program to those different types of channels or introduce new retail concepts.

- Transportation and physical distribution issues are critically important in global marketing because of the geographical distances involved in sourcing products and serving customers in different parts of the world.

- Today, many companies are reconfiguring their supply chains to cut costs and improve efficiency.

[Chapter Fourteen] – Global Advertising

- Marketing communications – the promotion P of the marketing mix – includes advertising, public relations, sales promotion and personal selling.

- Although marketers may identify opportunities for global advertising campaigns, local adaptation or distinct local campaigns may also required.

- A powerful reason to try to create a global campaign is that the process forces a company to attempt to identify a global market for its product.

- In addition, the identification of global appeals and benefits forces a company to probe deeply to identify basic needs and buying motives.

- When creating advertising, care must be taken to ensure that the art direction and copy are appropriate for the intended audiences in target countries.

- Advertisers may place a single global agency in charge of worldwide advertising; it is also possible to use one or more agencies on a regional or local basis. Advertising intensity varies from country to country.

- The United States, for example, accounts less than 25 per cent of gross world product but almost 50 per cent of world advertising expenditures.

- Media availability varies considerably from country to country. Television is the leading medium in many markets but its availability for advertising is severely restricted or non-existent in others.

[Chapter Fifteen] – Global Promotion

- Marketing communications – the promotion P of the marketing mix – includes advertising, public relations, personal selling, sales promotion, direct marketing, trade shows and sponsorship.

- These techniques are important tools in global marketing. Public relations are important tools in global marketing.

- Public relations are important in global marketing. Corporate communications must be designed to foster goodwill and provide accurate, timely information, especially in the event of a crisis.

- Personal selling or one-on-one communication requires company representatives to be well versed in the culture of countries in which they do business.

- Behaviour in each stage of the selling process may have to be appropriately tailored to individual country measurement.

- Sales promotion must also conform to regulations in each country markets. An ill-designed promotion can result in unwanted publicity and lost customers.

- Other considerations for the international marketing mix are direct marketing trade shows, sponsorship and Internet.

- Each technique is rapidly gaining acceptance around the world and can alter a company's marketing strategies for directly reaching the consumer.

[Chapter Sixteen] – Global E-Marketing

- The rapid advances in information technology are profoundly affecting the way global marketing is conducted.

- The global, instant reach of customers has not only opened up additional distribution and communication channels and enabled precise targeting (segment of one), customisation and interaction but has also given rise to fundamentally new business models.

- Technologies changes have also empowered customers by providing more transparency, allowing them to propose their own prices, and offering a platform for dealing directly with each other at auction sites.

- The need to reach a dominant market position in a very short time, the shift up from firm focused strategies to strategic alliances and networks, high start-up investment requirements and the heightened importance of ongoing innovations are amongst the issues raised in this context.

- Finally, we have taken a closer look at the components of the electronic value chain to demonstrate the different roles global marketers can play in e-commerce.

[Chapter Seventeen] – Leading, Organising and Monitoring the Global Marketing Effort

- To respond to the opportunities and threats in the global marketing environment, a firm must have a global vision and strategy.

- By providing leadership, organising global effort and establishing control procedures, a firm can exploit global opportunities.

- Leaders must have the vision, in addition to the technical resources, to build global competencies.

- In organising the global marketing effort, a structure that enables the company to respond to relevant differences in international market environments and enables the company to extend valuable corporate knowledge is the goal.

- A balance between autonomy and integration must be established. Within this organisation, firms must establish core competencies to be competitive.

- For global marketing control practices to be effective, differences in purely domestic control must be recognised and implemented in planning and control practices.

[Chapter Eighteen] – The Future of Global Marketing

- The future of global marketing will reflect five major changes in world growth but with some major new directions.

- The growth of Southeast Asia has been interrupted. That region now offers exceptional risk and reward equations for global marketers who are willing to make a bet on the long-term potential of the region.

- The cost of market entry has dropped as dramatically as the decline in values of national currencies.

- For companies with a stomach for risk, there is an opportunity to invest, building market positions in countries that most experts believe will soon return to long-term growth.

- In the meantime, other world regions will continue to grow, and world wealth will become more evenly distributed.

- The trade cycle has not eliminated manufacturing as a source of employment and income countries.

- By investing in capital equipment and by designing products for manufacturability, rich countries have proven that they can continue to successfully compete as manufacturing locations.

- Global markets will continue to grow in importance as global marketers continue their quests to identify and serve global segments.

- This growth will enhance and expand the value of global experience for managers and executives worldwide.

- Finally, marketing is at the threshold of a new and exciting era: e-business, e-commerce and e-marketing.

- For the first time in history, marketers have the tools to address the needs of the individual customer.

PART 2 – FOREIGN EXCHANGE MANAGEMENT

[Chapter One] – International Monetary System

- There are various theories which have been propounded for explaining the reasons behind the international trade.

- There have been movements in the exchange rate over period and the movements are called the International Monetary System.

- The experiments with various kinds of monetary systems have shown us that there is no perfect monetary system.

- Each system has its drawbacks as well as positive points. Each system involves an adjustment mechanism, which has to be allowed to work to make the system last.

- The most important we learn is that the monetary system should be allowed to evolve as a response to the changing environment, while maintaining some level of stability.

- How can this balance be achieved in open question to which countries and supranational institutions are still trying to find an answer?

[Chapter Two] – Foreign Exchange Market

- There are a number of intricacies involved in the operations of the foreign exchange market.

- There is a regulatory authority which ensures the smooth functioning of the markets through regulating their operations to an extent by the forex market around the world.

- The operations and regulatory framework understanding of the markets are essential for a finance manager for managing foreign currency risk for the firm.

- Another important aspect is the inter linkages amongst the various financial markets (money markets, real markets and forex markets).

[Chapter Three] – Exchange Rate Determination

- The market forces, if left free, would have the potential to bring the prices of various commodities (including money) in line, internationally, with various practical factors that impede the process.

- As a result, prices, interest rates and exchange rates are across countries, which do not fall in line with the parity conditions.

- Despite these factors, a long-term trend is observed whereby the various variables are generally seen moving towards the parities.

- Hence, these parities are also considered along with other factors by the market players, while trying to forecast exchange rates.

[Chapter Four] – Exchange Rate Forecasting

- Different models of exchange rate determination predict different effects of changes in various economic variables on the exchange rates.

- Though conflicting, all these effects are observed in real-life situations. The final effect of a change in an economic variable is a combination of predictions of the various theories and is also dependent on the situation of the moment.

- Though this makes exchange rate forecasting a Herculean, the forecast made using economic indicators do help in having a long-term view, which is supplemented by technical analysis, which helps in having a short-term view.

[Chapter Five] – Introduction to Exchange Risk

- Corporate companies, whether operating domestically or internationally, are exposed to risks of adverse movement in profits resulting from movements in exchange rates.

- Foreign risk results when the domestic currency value of asset, liabilities or operating incomes becomes variable in response to unexpected changes in exchange rates. The variabilities are exchange rates and exposure.

- The variability above which are not exposed to rate changes create any exchange risk. Where exposure is measurable in terms of the slope of regression equation between exchange rate movements and changes in the values of assets or liabilities, exchange rate risk can be expressed as a function of exposure and variance of exchange rate.

- The price flexibility enjoyed by a firm is largely a factor of the price elasticity of demand. Price flexibility is negatively correlated to price elasticity, that is, the more the price elastic demand, the less the flexibility the firm enjoys to change the foreign currency price in case of a firm facing competition from imported goods and the domestic price remains unchanged.

- The price elasticity of demand depends on degree of competition, location of competitors and degree of product differentiation.

- There are various kinds of instruments that are firm to hedge itself against these exposures like forwards, future, options and swaps. These instruments are together called derivatives.

[Chapter Six] – Management of Exchange Risk

- There are a number of ways in which transaction and translation exposures can be managed. Though there is no perfect method, each one has its own feature, advantages and disadvantages which makes it suitable for particular situation.

- The strategies for managing operating exposure outlined above would prove to be effective if the exchange rate movements and their effects on operating profit could be predicted.

- But managing exposure is all about managing unpredictable exchange rate movements and their unpredictable effects on the operating profits of a company.

- This requires advance planning by the firm which involves a study of the possible exchange rate scenario and the probability that could be attached to them.

- It further involves estimating the effect of each scenario on the firm's operating profits and planning the possible corrective actions that would need to be taken in such scenario.

- It is top management which is involved for managing operating exposure.

- While implementing a policy for hedging operating exposure is extremely difficult in practice due to the continuously changing exchange rates, the difficulty is in predicting their effects from firms operating profit and the cost of input that goes in decision-making process.

- These costs and difficulties in implementation which makes the expected return will make it imperative that these activities should be undertaken only when the cost of leaving the exposed to exchange rate movements are expected to be large.

CONCLUSION

- This additional book under <u>MBA Basics in 24 Hours</u> helps you to get quick knowledge of Global Marketing and Foreign Trade Management.
- Short, simple summary & keywords can be used to present the whole topic in just less than three hours.
- The ideas and definitions can be used for examinations, viva and also knowledge sharing/transfer.
- Group discussions can be arranged and the above chapters are really helpful to bring out the best member in management.
- Examination papers can be set at the required levels in simple terms.
- The given information in all the chapters can also be used in schools, colleges and any other levels.
- Other eight books under 'MBA Basics in 24 hours' are also given in the same way to help out best for students and tutors (published in Amazon).

- Principles & Practices of Management
- Human Resource Management
- Financial Management
- Marketing Management
- Organisational Behaviour
- Managerial Economics
- Strategic Management
- Management Information Systems

For any feedback, query or suggestions please mail to astronara@gmail.com or info@zodiacservices.net.

You can also contact via www.zodiacservices.net/contact.

THANK YOU!

www.ingramcontent.com/pod-product-compliance
Lightning Source LLC
Chambersburg PA
CBHW030740180526
45157CB00008BA/3253